YOUR PASSPORT TO

PERU

Ryan Gale

raintree
a Capstone company — publishers for children

Raintree is an imprint of Capstone Global Library Limited, a company incorporated in England and Wales having its registered office at 264 Banbury Road, Oxford, OX2 7DY – Registered company number: 6695582

www.raintree.co.uk
myorders@raintree.co.uk

Edited by Jamie Hudalla
Designed by Colleen McLaren
Original illustrations © Capstone Global Library Limited 2021
Originated by Capstone Global Library Ltd
Printed and bound in India

978 1 3982 0557 4 (hardback)
978 1 3982 0558 1 (paperback)

British Library Cataloguing in Publication Data
A full catalogue record for this book is available from the British Library.

Acknowledgements
We would like to thank the following for permission to reproduce photographs: AP Images: Giancarlo Ávila/Grupo El Comercio, 13; iStockphoto: Nastasic, 10; Red Line Editorial: 5; Shutterstock Images: Anton_Ivanov, 6, CP DC Press, 27, Filip Bjorkman, cover (map), Izabela23, 9, J Duggan, 28, Jo Reason, 15, Mark Green, 22, Milton Rodriguez, cover (bottom), Noradoa, 16, Peruvian Art, cover (flag), Skreidzeleu, 18, SL-Photography, 25, studiolaska, 21 Design Elements: iStockphoto, Shutterstock Images

We would like to thank José Antonio Mazzotti, PhD, Professor of Spanish Culture and Civilization and Professor of Latin American Studies, at Tufts University, Massachusetts, USA, for his assistance in the preparation of this book.

Every effort has been made to contact copyright holders of material reproduced in this book. Any omissions will be rectified in subsequent printings if notice is given to the publisher.

CONTENTS

Words in **bold** are in the glossary.

CHAPTER ONE

WELCOME TO PERU!

Stone **ruins** sit on top of a rocky peak. Mountains and **tropical** forests surround the area. The ruins are part of the Inca city of Machu Picchu. It is in southern Peru. More than 1 million people visit Machu Picchu every year. It is one of many historic sites in Peru.

Peru is the third-largest country in western South America. More than 31 million people live there. The **native** Inca people once ruled there. But the Spanish **colonized** the region in the 1500s. Both native and Spanish cultures have influenced Peru's buildings, foods and traditions.

SIGHTS IN PERU

Peru has coastline and dry plains in the west. A tropical rainforest covers the east. The Andes Mountains lie in between.

MAP OF PERU

Andes
Mountains

PERU

■ Capital City
● City
⬡ Landform
▲ Landmark
★ Park
◆ Attraction

Caral

LIMA

Manú
National Park

Machu Picchu

Islas Ballestas
National Reserve

Cuzco ●

Nazca Lines

Colca
Canyon

Arequipa

N
W   E
S

Explore Peru's cities
and landmarks.

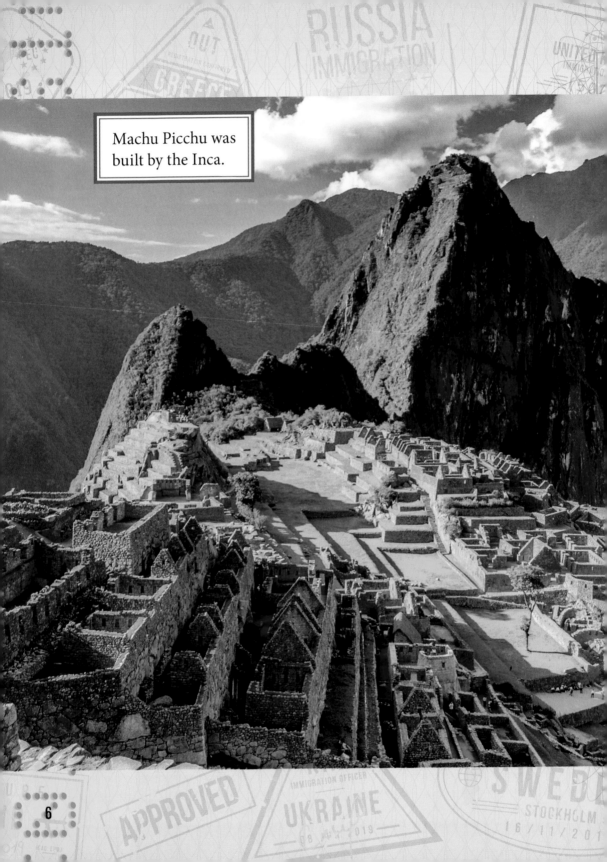

Machu Picchu was built by the Inca.

FACT FILE

NAME: .... REPUBLIC OF PERU
POPULATION: 31,914,989
LAND AREA: .... 1,285,216 SQ. KM (798,596 SQ. MI)
CAPITAL: .... LIMA
MONEY: .... SOL
GOVERNMENT: .... DEMOCRATIC REPUBLIC
LANGUAGE: .... SPANISH, QUECHUA AND AYMARA
GEOGRAPHY: Located in western South America, Peru is bordered by Ecuador, Colombia, Brazil, Bolivia and Chile.
NATURAL RESOURCES: Peru has fish, coal, gas, wood and gold.

Peru's West Coast brushes against the Pacific Ocean. These waters are home to dolphins, penguins and many types of fish. Tourists can see whales on whale-watching tours. They can also visit the beaches along the coast.

CHAPTER TWO

HISTORY OF PERU

People have lived in Peru for thousands of years. Cave paintings in southern Peru date back 7,000 years. The city of Caral is in western Peru. The Norte Chico, an ancient people, built it 5,000 years ago. It is one of the oldest cities in South America.

THE INCA

The Inca people ruled Peru between the 1100s and 1500s **CE**. They built hundreds of **pyramids**. Some may have been places to worship Inca gods. Rulers possibly used others to govern people. The Inca built roads. The roads helped them move goods and armies quickly. Pachacuti was the ninth Inca ruler. He used his armies to take control of other lands. The Inca **Empire** became the largest in South America.

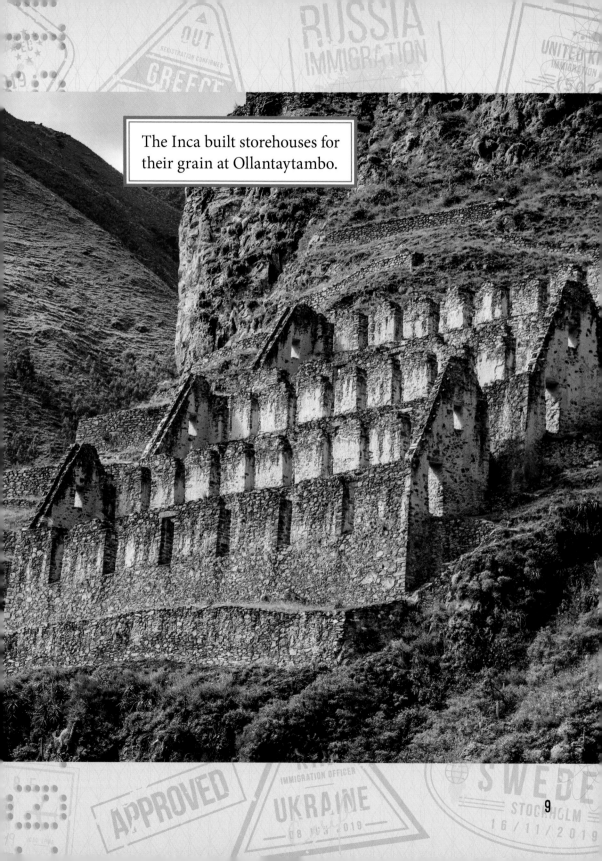

The Inca built storehouses for their grain at Ollantaytambo.

Conquistadors stole valuable items from the tombs in Huaca Rajada.

THE SPANISH

Spanish explorer Francisco Pizarro visited Peru in 1526. He saw a country rich in gold and silver. He returned in 1532 with a small army of Spanish soldiers called **conquistadors**. They destroyed the Inca empire.

FACT

The Inca had no alphabet. They spoke the Quechua language. It is still spoken in Peru today.

GUANO

Peru became famous for its guano in the 1840s. Guano is bird droppings. The islands off the coast of Peru used to be home to countless birds. Tonnes of guano had built up on the islands over hundreds of years. Guano contains nitrates, which help plants grow. People mined the guano. They shipped it to Europe and North America. Farmers used it to grow crops in areas with poor soil.

TIMELINE OF PERUVIAN HISTORY

2000s BCE: The city of Caral is built.

1100s CE: The Inca people live in Peru.

1532: The Spanish conquer the Inca.

1780: People in Peru rebel against Spain.

1824: The people of Peru win independence from Spain.

1968–1975: Juan Velasco Alvarado becomes **dictator** of Peru.

1979: Peru creates a **constitution** that limits the president's power.

2018: Martín Vizcarra becomes president.

People from Spain colonized Peru after defeating the Inca. The Spanish forced native Peruvians to work in mines and give up their language and religion. Peruvians learned to speak Spanish. Many Peruvians were forced to become Christians.

The people of Peru rebelled against Spain in 1780. But they were not able to win their freedom until 1824. Peru's leaders struggled to form a stable government.

Martín Vizcarra started his political career in 2006.

A CHANGE IN POWER

In 1968, a military leader called Juan Velasco Alvarado took control of the country. He became a dictator. Seven years later, other military commanders overthrew him. Peru created a new constitution in 1979. It limited the power of rulers. It also gave people more voting rights. Another constitution was created in 1993. Citizens now elect a president every five years. Martín Vizcarra became president in 2018.

CHAPTER THREE

EXPLORE PERU

Peru has amazing natural areas. The Amazon rainforest covers 60 per cent of the country. It is home to many plants, such as orchids and lupuna trees. Animals such as spider monkeys and jaguars roam the forest. Some native peoples live there too.

NATURAL SITES

The Amazon River begins in Peru. It flows into the Atlantic Ocean. The river is about 6,400 kilometres (4,000 miles) long. This makes it the second-longest river in the world.

Much of Peru's West Coast is desert. Peru's two largest cities are Lima and Arequipa. They are on the west coast. The deserts spread to the foot of the Andes Mountains. The Andes stretch from the north-west to the south-east of Peru. The Andes is the longest mountain range in the world. People walk and climb the mountains.

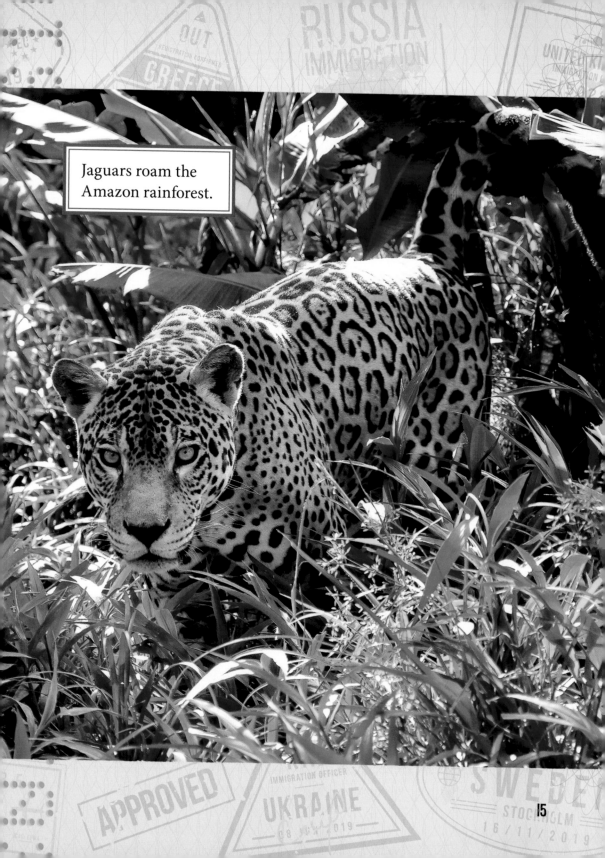

Jaguars roam the
Amazon rainforest.

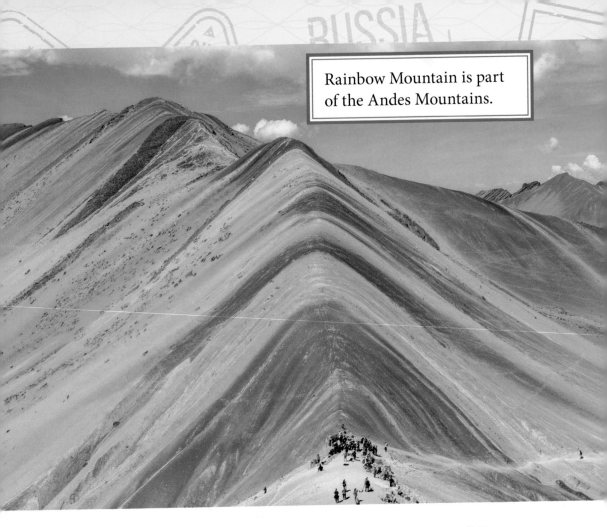

Rainbow Mountain is part of the Andes Mountains.

People can explore Colca Canyon in the Andes. It plunges more than 3,048 metres (10,000 feet) deep. The Colca River flows along the bottom. Tourists canoe down this river. Others walk or cycle along the top of the canyon.

FACT

Peru has more than 1,800 species of birds.

WILDLIFE

People visit Peru's national parks to see wildlife. Manú National Park is the largest. It includes parts of the Andes and the Amazon rainforest. It has the most plant and animal species of any one place on Earth.

The Islas Ballestas National Reserve stretches across the south-western coast of Peru. It is made up of several islands. Many sea creatures, including sea lions and penguins, live there. People can watch humpback whales swim along the northern coast of Peru between August and October. That is when the whales reach Peru from Antarctica, where they spend the summer.

FACT

The rainforest has many types of plants. Some can be used to treat illnesses. Scientists study the plants to find ones that might help people who are ill.

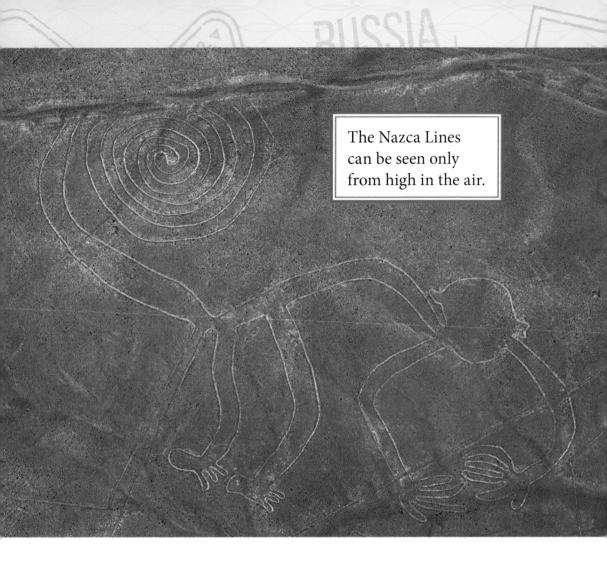

The Nazca Lines can be seen only from high in the air.

HISTORICAL SITES

Peru has famous historical sites that have become ruins. Machu Picchu is the most famous of these. The Inca built the city of Machu Picchu. They created it on top of a mountain. Historians think this may have helped protect the city from its enemies. Other ruins in Peru date back to a time before the Inca.

Peru is also famous for the Nazca Lines. These are drawings that the ancient Nazca people cut into the ground. Many are images of plants and animals. Some of them are very large. They can only be seen while flying above them. Some historians believe that the drawings may have been used to send messages to Nazca gods. Others think they were a form of calendar.

EXCITING CITIES

There is beautiful **architecture** in Peru's cities. Lima, Peru's capital, is known for its Spanish-style buildings. These buildings often feature **stucco** walls and tiled roofs. The Huaca Pucllana ruins are in Lima. This pyramid was built of clay bricks more than 1,000 years ago.

The city of Cuzco sits among the Andes Mountains. It was the capital of the Inca Empire. Tourists can still see Inca ruins in Cuzco. The city is packed with food stalls, craft markets and old Spanish churches.

CHAPTER FOUR

DAILY LIFE

Many Peruvians live and work in cities. There are usually more jobs in cities than in the countryside. Children between the ages of 7 and 16 go to school. Classes usually begin at 8.00 a.m. They end at 2.00 p.m.

People treat lunch as the biggest meal of the day. They often take a short nap after lunch. This is called a siesta. Many businesses close during lunch and siesta time. Businesses typically stay open until 8.00 or 9.00 p.m. This means people often eat dinner late in the evening.

LIFE IN THE COUNTRY

Many people who live in the country are farmers. They grow potatoes, corn, rice and other crops. They also keep chickens, pigs and other animals for food. Some people keep sheep, llamas and alpacas for their wool. They sell the wool or use it to make clothing.

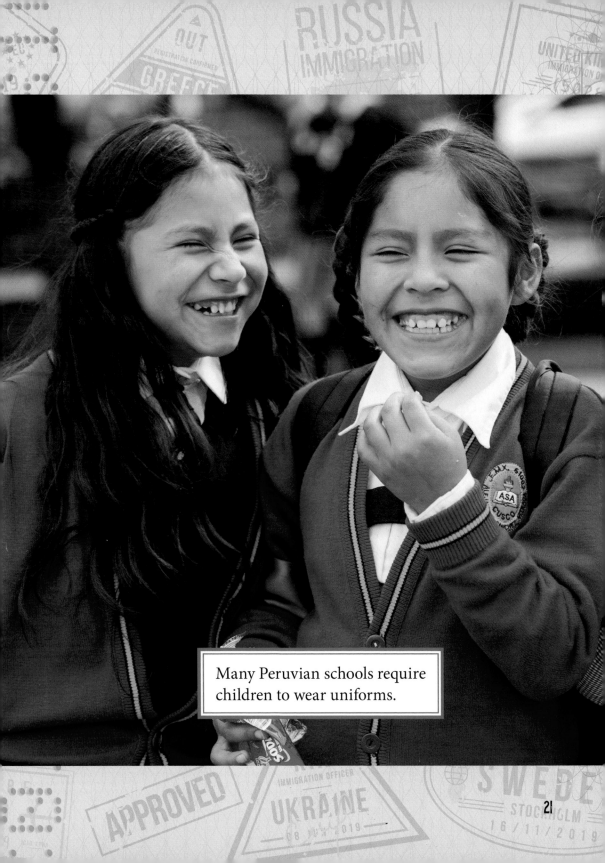

Many Peruvian schools require children to wear uniforms.

Quechua women often wear clothes with bright patterns.

A VARIETY OF FOODS

Peruvians eat different foods depending on where they live. People who live near the coast eat a lot of seafood. People who live in the highlands tend to eat meat, corn and potatoes. Soups are popular in Peru. They are often made with spicy peppers. Dishes made with rice and quinoa are also popular.

LIMONADA

A lot of limes are grown in Peru. Drinks with lime in them, like *limonada*, are popular there. With the help of an adult, you can make *limonada* at home.

Ingredients:
- 2 limes, quartered and seeds removed
- 2 litres cold water
- 100 g granulated sugar
- Ice cubes

Method:

1. Place the limes, sugar and half of the water in a blender. Blend until the limes are crushed.
2. Strain the lime mixture and add the remaining half of the water.
3. Serve with or without ice.

TRADITIONAL DRESS

Some of Peru's native people wear traditional clothing. This often includes brightly coloured coats. They also wear woolly hats and ponchos. Ponchos are a type of cloak often made from a blanket. They keep people warm high in the mountains, where it is cold.

FACT

Women living in the Andes Mountains wear traditional hats called *monteras*. The women decorate the hats with beads, flowers and sequins.

CHAPTER FIVE

HOLIDAYS AND CELEBRATIONS

The people of Peru enjoy native and religious holidays. Peruvians celebrate Independence Day on 28 July. Peru declared its freedom from Spain on that day in 1824. Some businesses and homes hang up Peru's flag for the whole month of July.

The Inca Festival of the Sun is held in Cuzco. It honours the Inca sun god, Inti. It begins on 24 June and lasts for a whole week. People recreate Inca ceremonies during this time. The ceremonies often include music and traditional costumes.

RELIGIOUS HOLIDAYS

About 60 per cent of Peruvians are Catholic. Christmas and Easter are important holidays for Peruvian Catholics. The season of Carnival is also important.

People celebrate the Inca Festival of the Sun by dancing.

Carnival takes place in February or March. There are parades and parties. Carnival leads up to Lent. Lent is a period of 40 days. Many Catholics don't eat meat or certain other foods during this time.

CHAPTER SIX

SPORT AND RECREATION

Football is the most popular sport in Peru. Many children play football at school. The Estadio Monumental stadium in Lima is the largest football stadium in South America. It can hold more than 80,000 people. Volleyball and golf are also popular sports in Peru.

BULLFIGHTING

Bullfighting was once a big tradition in Peru. It is still practised in some parts of the country. Bullfighting involves people called matadors. They wear bright costumes and carry swords or spears. They enter a ring with a bull and try to avoid being hit. The fight ends when the matadors kill the bull. But many people have stopped watching bullfighting. It is harmful to animals.

Paolo Guerrero is considered to be one of Peru's best footballers.

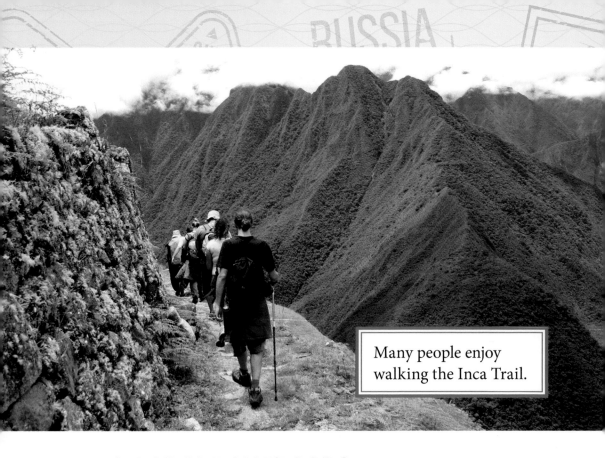

Many people enjoy
walking the Inca Trail.

THE GREAT OUTDOORS

There are many outdoor activities to enjoy in Peru.
The Andes Mountains are popular with climbers.
Many walk the Inca Trail. This 42-kilometre (26-mile)
trip starts outside Cuzco and ends at Machu Picchu.

Some people like to ride dune buggies in the desert.
Dune buggies are four-wheeled vehicles that climb
mounds of sand. Sand surfing is a fun desert sport.
People slide down a sand dune on a surfboard.

JUEGO DE SAPO

Sapo is a popular children's game in Peru. The game comes from an Inca legend about a magical sapo, or frog. People threw pieces of gold at frogs. They believed that if the frog caught a piece of gold in its mouth, it would grant a wish. To play, they use coins or tokens and a box with holes on the top. A toy frog with its mouth open is placed on the box.

1. Players take turns throwing coins at the box.
2. If a player throws a coin in a hole, he or she gains a point.
3. If a player manages to throw a coin into the toy frog's mouth, he or she is an instant winner!

People also surf the waves on the Pacific Ocean. Some people go rafting on rivers in the Amazon rainforest. It is a good way to see animals and birds. From surfing dunes and waves to visiting ancient pyramids, Peru has activities for everyone to enjoy.

THE BIRTHPLACE OF SURFING

Some people think surfing began in Polynesia. Others think surfing started in Peru. Fishers in Peru have used small boats made of reeds for hundreds of years. Their boats look similar to surfboards. Ancient paintings and clay pots also show people riding waves. People in Peru still use reed boats for fishing and surfing.

GLOSSARY

architecture
art of practice of
designing buildings

BCE/CE
BCE means Before
Common Era, or before
year one. CE means
Common Era, or after
year one.

colonize
take control of a
foreign country

conquistador
16th-century military
leader from Spain

constitution
system of laws that state the
rights of the people and the
powers of the government

dictator
leader who has complete
control over a country

empire
large area ruled by
an emperor

native
born in a particular
country or place; also, tied
to a certain location

pyramid
structure with a square
base and four triangular
walls that meet in a point at
the top

ruins
remains of an
ancient structure

stucco
layer of cement and sand
coating the outside of a wall

tropical
climate that is very hot
and humid

FIND OUT MORE

BOOKS

Geography Matters in the Inca Empire (Geography Matters in Ancient Civilizations), Melanie Waldron (Raintree, 2016)

Investigating Machu Picchu (Graphic Expeditions), Emily Sohn (Raintree, 2011)

Rainforests (Flowchart Science: Habitats and Ecosystems), Louise and Richard Spilsbury (Raintree, 2020)

WEBSITES

kids.nationalgeographic.com/explore/countries/peru
Find out more about Peru with National Geographic.
I did

www.bbc.co.uk/bitesize/clips/zc6mhyc
Watch this BBC Bitesize clip that compares life in two different Peruvian villages.

www.dkfindout.com/uk/history/incas/machu-picchu
Learn more about Machu Picchu.

INDEX

OTHER BOOKS IN THIS SERIES

YOUR PASSPORT TO CHINA
YOUR PASSPORT TO ECUADOR
YOUR PASSPORT TO EL SALVADOR
YOUR PASSPORT TO ETHIOPIA
YOUR PASSPORT TO FRANCE
YOUR PASSPORT TO IRAN
YOUR PASSPORT TO KENYA
YOUR PASSPORT TO RUSSIA
YOUR PASSPORT TO SPAIN